# This.
[A]

# Is
[F]

# A.
[A#]

# Book.
[A#]

# With.
## [C]

# One.
[D]

# Hundred.
[D#]

# Pages.
[F]

# 9.
[F]

# 10.
[F]

# Eleven.
## [F#]

# 12.
[G#]

# 13.
[A#]

# Keep.
[A#]

# Going.
[A#]

# You're.
[G#]

# Almost.
## [F#]

# There.
[G#]

# 19.
[F#]

# 20.
[F]

# Is.
[F]

# This.
[D#]

# A.
[D#]

# Puzzle.
[F]

?
[F#]

# 26.
[F]

# 27. [D#]

# 28.
[C#]

# Don't. [C#]

# Forget.
[D#]

# To.
[F]

# Floss.
## [D#]

# Thirty-three.
## [C#]

# Technically.
[C]

# That.
[D]

# Was.
[E]

# Two.
[G]

# Words.
## [F]

# But.
[F]

# What's.
[F]

# The.
[F]

# Count.
[F]

# Now.
[F]

?
[F]

# 45.
[F]

# 46.
## [F]

# 47.

# Are.

# You.

# Still.

# Here.

?

# 53.

Got.

# To.

# Hand.

# It.

To.

# You.

For.

# Keeping.

# Up.

# With.

# The.

# Pages.

# 66.

# 67.

# 68.

# Sixty-Nine.

# 70.

Did.

You.

# Crack.

The.

# Code.

Yet.

?

# 78.

# Think.

# 80.

# About.

82.

It.

# 84.

# 85.

You.

Should.

Probably.

# Check.

# Reddit.

For.

This.

# One.

94.

# Coming.

# To.

# An.

End.

!

# 100
*G F# D# A G# E G#*

www.ingramcontent.com/pod-product-compliance
Lightning Source LLC
Chambersburg PA
CBHW021451210526
45463CB00002B/733